Haunted Houses

OTHER TITLES IN THE SERIES:

The Mysterious  & Unknown

Haunted Houses

by Stuart A. Kallen

San Diego, CA

For more information, contact
ReferencePoint Press, Inc.
PO Box 27779
San Diego, CA 92198
www.ReferencePointPress.com

Picture credits: AP/Wide World Photos, 69
Dreamstime, 36, 46, 52, 54
Fortean Picture Library, 21, 83, 86
Stuart A. Kallen, 17, 33, 37, 40, 62
North Wind Picture Archives, 9, 38

Series design and book layout:
Amy Stirnkorb

LIBRARY OF CONGRESS CATALOGING-IN-PUBLICATION DATA

Kallen, Stuart A., 1955-
  Haunted houses / by Stuart A. Kallen.
    p. cm. -- (The mysterious & unknown)
  Includes bibliographical references and index.
  ISBN-13: 978-1-60152-026-5 (hardback)
  ISBN-10: 1-60152-026-3 (hardback)
  1. Haunted houses--Juvenile literature. 2. Ghosts--Juvenile literature. I. Title.
  BF1475.K35 2007
  133.1'22--dc22

                                                                      2007020874

CONTENTS

FOREWORD

"Strange is our situation here upon earth."
—*Albert Einstein*

Since the beginning of recorded history, people have been perplexed, fascinated, and even terrified by events that defy explanation. While science has demystified many of these events, such as volcanic eruptions and lunar eclipses, some continue to remain outside the scope of the provable. Do UFOs exist? Are people abducted by aliens? Can some people see into the future? These questions and many more continue to puzzle, intrigue, and confound despite the enormous advances of modern science and technology.

It is these questions, phenomena, and oddities that Reference-Point Press's *The Mysterious & Unknown* series is committed to exploring. Each volume examines historical and anecdotal evidence as well as the most recent theories surrounding the topic in debate. Fascinating primary source quotes from scientists, experts, and eyewitnesses, as well as in-depth sidebars further inform the text. Full-color illustrations and photos add to each book's visual appeal. Finally, source notes, a bibliography, and a thorough index provide further reference and research support. Whether for research or the curious reader, *The Mysterious & Unknown* series is certain to satisfy those fascinated by the unexplained.

INTRODUCTION

Not Home Alone

Writing in *The Haunted and the Haunters* in 1921, Sir Edward Bulwer-Lytton states, "It was not so much what [my wife and I] saw or heard . . . as it was an undefinable terror which seized both of us whenever we passed by the door of a certain unfurnished room, in which we neither saw nor heard anything."[1] Although Bulwer-Lytton was writing about a fictional haunted house, there are millions of people who can recognize his description of an indistinct horror found lurking in a haunted house. These folks are driven to distraction by things that go bump in the night, doors that slam when no wind blows, and ghostly whispers of restless phantoms calling from beyond the grave.

Many people do not believe in such phenomena, but they are a minority in the United States. According to a 2003 Harris poll, 51 percent of Americans believe in ghosts and apparitions. In Great Britain, perhaps the most haunted island in the world, the percentage is even higher. A poll conducted by retailer Choice UK found that 68 percent of the British population believes that haunted houses are real, and 12 percent say they have seen ghosts in their own houses or in the homes of friends or relatives. It is little wonder then that haunted huts, houses, mansions, and castles

are said to exist all over the world.

In Jamaica, the ghost of slave owner Annie Porter haunts Rose Hall near Montego Bay. She is known as "the White Witch of Rose Hall." Although the former plantation house is now a luxury hotel, Porter can still be seen in a green velvet dress, riding the grounds on a large black horse, and flaying her whip at anyone unfortunate enough to be caught in her path. On certain nights the walls of Rose Hall can be heard groaning with the cries of slaves whom the White Witch tortured to death in the 1700s.

Halfway around the world, the Penrith House near Sydney was once the site of unspeakable crimes committed by members of the Australian mafia. Although the house has been abandoned for years and has no electrical service, lights turn on in a tower and a white shaded figure comes down to visit those who stray onto the property.

In some places, local inhabitants have developed elaborate rituals to clear houses of spirits like these. On the Pacific island of New Guinea, residents believe that ghosts of the newly dead haunt their old homes and possibly cause disease or death to those still living there. To obtain the goodwill of the ghosts, relatives offer sacrificial gifts such as butchered pigs. They also sometimes place masks, costumes, and feathers in the surrounding forest, hoping the ghosts will search for the items and lose their way. A similar practice takes place in Siberia, where corpses might be taken on a twisting, winding route to the graveyard to confuse the spirits of the dead so that they will forget the way back home.

Not all cultures try to evict phantoms from their haunted habitats. In Old English, the word *ghost* means "guest," and many in the British Isles accept the idea that their homes are haunted

While some ghosts tend to appear on their own, others, like this ghost, can be summoned by mediums.

by apparitions. Oftentimes these apparitions appear as foggy masses of smoke, flashes of light, or semivisible and vaporous human entities. Many are distant relatives of modern residents and are treated with the same respect and deference that they had received in life. This is despite the fact that the ghosts may occasionally howl in the night, walk through walls at inopportune moments, or emit repulsive smells at dinnertime.

While the British seem unusually tolerant of their phantoms, in most cases those who live in haunted houses experience terror, alarm, trepidation, long-term psychological damage, or even death. As St. John D. Seymour and Harry L. Neligan explain in *True Irish Ghost Stories*:

> There is something very eerie in being shut up within the four walls of a house with a ghost. The poor human being is placed at such a disadvantage. If we know that a gateway, or road, or field has the reputation of being haunted, we can . . . make a detour, and so avoid the unpleasant locality. But the presence of a ghost in a house creates a very different state of affairs. It appears and disappears at its own sweet will, with a total disregard for our feelings: it seems to be as much part and parcel of the domicile as the staircase or the hall door, and, consequently, nothing short of leaving the house or of pulling it down (both of these solutions are not always practicable) will free us absolutely from the unwelcome presence.[2]

"There is something very eerie in being shut up within the four walls of a house with a ghost."

— St. John D. Seymour and Harry L. Neligan explain why those who live in haunted houses can suffer psychological damage.

CHAPTER 1

Who Haunts Houses?

There has long been speculation that the portal leading from life to death is not a one-way passage. While thousands of people depart from the world of the living on a daily basis, it seems those on the other side can occasionally exit the domain of the dead. Sometimes they get caught in the middle, neither living nor dead. Through some mystery of time and space, they are able to reanimate in the realm of earthly existence and inhabit the homes of the living. Perhaps this is why some in the Fiji Islands remove the dead from their homes through windows or even holes cut into the walls. The islanders do not want the ghosts to remember the location of the door, move back in, and haunt those who remain behind.

Elsewhere, though, all types of homes have become centers for supernatural occurrences and paranormal phenomena. These domiciles may contain a wide assortment of weird and enigmatic spirits, but they most often fall into three categories: ghosts, poltergeists, and demons.

All in the Family

Ghosts are by far the most commonly sighted specters in houses that are haunted. Simply defined, ghosts are entities that continue to walk the earth after death. These ghosts, also known as revenants, may appear as visible only to a single living person or to specifically chosen people, called percipients. For example, Prince Michael of Greece, author of *Living with Ghosts*, writes that his father, Prince Christopher, once saw the reflection of a ghost in the bedroom window of his castle. The apparition was a woman dressed in antiquated clothing with a mask partially covering her face. While Prince Christopher quickly understood the woman to be a ghost, his valet, who was standing nearby, saw nothing. Days later, at another royal castle, the prince happened to discover an old painting of the ghostly woman holding the mask in her hand. As Prince Michael writes, the revenant only appears for specific people:

> She was an ancestor of the . . . owner of the house; she had been incarcerated by her husband, who was mad with jealousy of her great beauty. The unfortunate prisoner sought to throw herself on the mercy of the king: in vain, for she died a prisoner. Since then, she was supposed to appear periodically to the descendants of the kings . . . still forlornly seeking their aid.[3]

Revenants seeking specific percipients are not limited to royalty. It is often the case that apparitions will make themselves

known to their living spouses, other family members, or friends. Sometimes, these ghosts are delusions conceived in grief by the living. For example, a widow might imagine seeing the ghost of her deceased husband long after he passed into the dimension of the dead.

Haunting All and Sundry

Many ghosts are seemingly less particular about whom they haunt. Unlike revenants who left the earth but returned from the dead, these ghosts never completely entered the world of the dead. Although not among the living, they occupy a mysterious dimension between life and death where some part of their spirit or image continues to occupy the earth. This type of haunter may be seen by various people over the years. Most of the percipients in such cases are unfamiliar with the apparitions. They are simply thought of as anonymous spirits from a long-lost era. In such instances the phantasms do not target the percipients with any particular message and may in fact be completely unaware of their existence. These ghosts just happen to haunt a house, have done so for years, and will continue to do so in the future no matter who lives there. Oftentimes they are wearing the clothes in which they died. They might also exhibit distinct behavior, such as rattling chains, cackling loudly, or wielding a bloody sword. Such terrifying acts are repeated year after year, century after century. This type of ghost is most likely to cause fear, panic, and hysteria in the percipient since its arrival is unexpected, its visage is unrecognizable, and its motives are unknown.

Supernatural beings caught between life and death have played central roles in thousands of haunted-house stories. They may be desiccated old women in Victorian dresses holding fans

to their faces, Revolutionary War soldiers with tricornered hats waving the bloody stumps of missing limbs, or little girls in nightgowns clutching tattered teddy bears to their chests. Whatever the case, these troubled souls have a physical presence, or terrestrial substance, and percipients may hear, see, feel, or, in some cases, smell, the ghosts.

Why Do Ghosts Appear?

Why and when such ghosts appear is a subject of great mystery and debate. Some believe that when a person dies, he or she releases an electrical charge, electrons, or positive ions that are contained within the cells of the human body. This electrical emanation might be particularly strong in a person who is murdered or dies suddenly in an accident. The electrical waveforms purportedly remain in the air and reproduce a scene that can be viewed by people who are open to such perceptions.

Another theory postulates that ghosts are a result of a time slip, a brief opening in the dimension between the past and the present. When a time slip occurs, anyone nearby will get a glimpse into the past and see the person who inhabited the house in another age. This would explain the "echo" effect of many ghosts, where their behavior is repetitive, robotic, and unchanging. However, not all ghosts exhibit such echoes, and there are as many theories as to why they appear as there are stories to describe their antics. Confronting this reality, ghost-story author Marc Alexander writes in *Phantom Britain*, "As one gathers accounts of ghosts and compares them, the more one realizes that the only rule about them is that there is no rule. . . . The questions are endless, the answers so far are only speculative."[4]

Whatever the case, those who study supernatural phenomena

say most ghosts—up to 82 percent—are on some sort of mission. They may be completing unfinished business or calling attention to wrongdoing that went unpunished during their lifetime. Sometimes ghosts bring a message of looming death or disaster. Other times apparitions have a positive message, visiting the living to tell them that the afterlife is a fine place and further grieving is unnecessary.

Who Is Responsible for Apparition Appearances?

Whether a ghost is a long-dead revenant or a haunter with only one foot in the grave, it is often impossible to predict its behavior. Some appear regularly, others only on the rarest of occasions. It may be that specific percipients are responsible for ghosts appearing. These people summon ghosts, voluntarily or involuntarily, by sending out some sort of mysterious signal much as a radio transmitter broadcasts a song through invisible waves present in the air. The ghosts are drawn to the percipient's signal and appear. Hillary Evans explains in *Hauntings and Poltergeists*:

> The fact that some people see haunters and others don't encourages the view that there is a specific ghost-seeing faculty which may be either an ability which all humans possess though in varying degrees, or a talent which some people possess while others don't. There is an abundance of anecdotal testimony from other contexts of paranormal experience that some people are "psychically" gifted, enabling them to "see" or "sense" things that the majority cannot. . . . The alternative possibility

remains, that seeing or failing to see haunters may be a matter of circumstances, whose nature we can only guess at. It is even possible that *all* dead persons leave behind them a haunting component, but that only some—as it might be, those with sufficient motivation or will—are ever seen.[5]

An Evil Reputation

Another theory about apparition appearances concerns the haunted house itself. Some believe that houses and other buildings absorb ghostly energy and store it in unused rooms, attics, basements, and outdoor sheds. This theory addresses why it is mostly old buildings that are haunted. The damp, stale air of an abandoned room creates a perfect environment for all sorts of creepy creatures, including rats, snakes, spiders, and spirits. One such example comes from the haunted bedroom in the house at Number 50 Berkeley Square in London. This room was inhabited by a malevolent entity filled with hate.

According to reports in *Mayfair* magazine from 1879, Berkeley Square was a "house that had an evil reputation for being badly haunted."[6] The cause of this haunting was said to have begun in the late 1700s, when a man named Dupre used one of the house's upper bedrooms to confine his mentally deranged brother. The brother was so violent that he had to be fed his meals through a hole in the door. Upon his death, he became a vile ghost that forever haunted the bedroom and came to be known as "the Horror of Berkeley Square." The first person to suffer the wrath of the Horror was a maid who lived in the room in the 1830s. After a few hours in the room upon her first night in the house, according to *Mayfair*, "the household . . . was awakened by fearful screams from the new servant's room and she was found staring in the middle of the floor, rigid as a corpse, with hideously glaring eyes—she had suddenly become a hopeless and raving madwoman."[7]

The owners of the home closed off the room and lived without incident for a time. However, when a skeptical guest insisted on staying the night in the room to prove there was no such thing as a haunted room, he was found dead in the morning. The owners abandoned the house, and it remained uninhabited for many years. In the early 1870s a skeptic named Sir Robert Worboys met the

home's owner in a London club. Worboys insisted the house could not be inhabited by a malicious apparition. He agreed to spend a night in the room while several friends slept downstairs. Worboys brought a pistol with him and hung a bell on a string so he could notify his companions if he encountered trouble.

On the fateful night, Worboys retired to the room, one hand on his pistol, the other on his bell string. When the bell began ringing, Worboys's friend rushed to the upstairs room. Moments before entering, they heard a gunshot. They found Worboys on the bed, his face twisted into a horrid expression of sheer terror. Although they first thought he had shot himself, there were no visible wounds on the body, and it was later said that Worboys had died of fear.

Some believe that abandoned houses like this one absorb ghostly energy and store it in undisturbed rooms, attics, and bedrooms.

In the years that followed, Berkeley Square remained abandoned, but neighbors heard bizarre noises from the house, such as heavy objects being dragged across the wooden floors, bells ringing, windows and doors slamming, and inhuman screams. Then, on Christmas Eve 1878, two sailors on leave, Robert Martin and Edward Blunded, decided that the house on Berkeley Square looked like a perfect place to sleep after a drunken night on the town. Retiring to the haunted room, the men were soon attacked by a whitish ghost with outstretched arms bearing talons instead of hands. Martin escaped and found a policeman on a foggy street nearby. The two men returned to the house, but before they could enter, they heard an upstairs window break and a scream. This was followed by the sight of Blunded's body falling onto the spiked rails of the fence that surrounded the house. As the impaled sailor died, he was unable to explain what forced him to jump. As *Mayfair* stated, "dead men tell no tales."[8]

Destructive, Threatening, and Baffling Poltergeists

Oftentimes, wicked ghosts like the Horror of Berkeley Square are referred to as *poltergeists*, an old German word that simply means "noisy ghosts." Poltergeists are known to haunt houses by slamming windows and heaving furniture across a room. In most cases, poltergeists are not malicious, only annoying spirits that wish to convey messages to the living. As renowned parapsychologist and author Hans Holzer writes, poltergeists are "ghostly [entities] desperately trying to get attention for their plight from people in *this* world. Not to harm anyone, but to get people to notice their presence."[9] On rare occasions, however, poltergeists can seriously wound or even kill those who live in haunted houses.

Unlike revenants and haunters, which may or may not depend on percipients for their appearance, poltergeists are attracted to a specific type of energy. As Holzer explains:

> Young people at the border of their sexual awakening can be the *source* of the energy allowing the phenomena to occur, but so can mentally handicapped people of any age and sexually frustrated individuals of any age, consciously or unconsciously. . . . The originator, however, is not the youngster or the mentally handicapped older person: they are merely the source, tapped against their will.[10]

Like a ghost, a poltergeist tends to hover around a house where it is said to have left some earthly task unfinished. These noisy ghosts might also inhabit a house accidentally, haunting a residence that was built on the site of an ancient graveyard or battlefield. No matter what the case, poltergeists need a psychic entity, such as an adolescent or mentally disturbed adult, in order to supply them with energy to haunt. According to Holzer:

> This link between the physical energies of living persons and the usually demented minds of dead persons produces the physical phenomena known as poltergeist activities, which can be very destructive, sometimes threatening, sometimes baffling to those who do not understand the underlying causes. The purpose [of] these physical activities is always to get the attention of living persons or

Did You Know?

In most cases, poltergeists are not malicious, only annoying spirits that wish to convey messages to the living.

perhaps to annoy them for personal reasons. The mentality behind this phenomenon is somewhere between the psychotic and the infantile, but at all times far from emotionally and mentally normal.[11]

"A Very Ugly Experience"

Some sort of unexplained psychotic mentality was definitely at work in a home occupied by Bill and Margo Estes and their 2 sons, Josh, age 4, and Adam, 11. Bill was a sergeant in the army, and the Estes residence, one half of a duplex, was located on the army base at Fort Leonard Wood in Missouri. The troubles began in 1998, when Josh saw a man in his bedroom at 3 A.M. and started screaming uncontrollably. No man was found, but this ghostly appearance was the precursor of madness that was to follow.

Before long, lights began to mysteriously blink on and off although an electrician could find no cause for the problem. During this time, the two family dogs began acting strangely. The larger dog would block the stairway, trying to prevent family members from going upstairs to bed at night. The smaller dog often growled at the air, making menacing sounds at some invisible force.

In November 1998 the activity increased. One day Margo heard footsteps coming down the stairs and felt a cool breeze pass by her. Sounds such as footsteps are typical in haunted houses, but what followed two nights later revealed the existence of a demented poltergeist that could take control of family members. According to Margo, she awoke in the middle of the night and felt a presence enter her body. She said she suddenly felt superhuman strength and a wicked force inside her telling her to kill her husband: "[It] wanted me to tear his face off, and I could hear the voice telling me what to do, and I kept saying, 'No! No, I don't

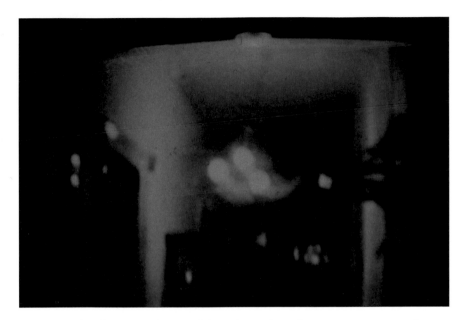

want to do that! No!' I could feel my hands moving towards my husband . . . it was a very ugly experience. . . . I was terrified and wanted to leave the house."[12]

The next night the poltergeist took control of Bill as he lay asleep in bed. Margo was still awake when Bill opened his eyes. His face twisted into an unfamiliar expression, and then he tried to strangle his wife. Margo screamed, and the force left Bill. He had no recollection of his crazed behavior.

The mysterious entity continued its grim deeds until the Estes family was driven from their home. Because the poltergeist only haunted that particular place, their problems were over. It is unknown if the force continued to haunt the occupants of the duplex in the years that followed. It might have been trying to create difficulty specifically for the Estes family or to deliver some sort of message. Or the poltergeist might have simply been a mischievous spirit tormenting the living for its own twisted pleasure.

Demons Hate Humans

While poltergeists are much less common than ghosts, demons are the rarest type of haunters. These supernatural spirits have long been associated with the devil, but demons have ostensibly existed for millennia. Ancient Hindu mythology from 5,000 years ago tells of aggressive ghostlike demons called *rakshasas* that can change shape and haunt the living. In the fourth century B.C., classical Greek philosopher Plato wrote of "independent [demons] who occupy a position somewhere between the human and the divine."[13] And ancient Jewish literature describes unclean demons that are dead souls occupying the world of the living.

Unlike ghosts, demons are not of human origin. However, demons can take possession of the mind and body of a human being. In such cases, exorcisms are conducted to free the victims of the satanic influence. Demons can also haunt houses; in order to do so, the evil spirits will impersonate ghosts or live among ghosts. Internet author SilverRain Queen explains:

> [Demons] do this for fun. . . . They can change into any form they choose to present themselves. Sometimes they are drawn to a house because the ghost of a person that died in a deep emotional state still resides and they like to "Lord" over them. Many times you hear stories where psychics come in and find several entities and one [the demon] that is very strong and emanates evil. He keeps [the ghosts] from crossing over.[14]

The demons come into the earthly world through caves or wells. Those that inhabit houses might crawl up through a sewer pipe or hole in the ground close to the haunted residence. Demonic behavior usually begins with small things, such as a faucet being turned on to drip in the middle of the night or scratching and thumping inside walls. As the haunting accelerates, demons try to foment terror in order to show the living that they are in control. They will strip the blankets from sleeping victims, shake beds violently, and knock items to the floor. Queen describes her experience with a demon haunting:

> Once they succeed in creating an atmosphere of fear [they] start to exaggerate their powers and then the personal attacks begin . . . scratches on the skin, slaps in the face. (I hate that one.) I've been slapped a few times alright. It progresses even more . . . to things swirling in the air, maybe he makes fire burst on the scene, voices can be heard. Sometimes he can even make himself known with an audible voice . . . [although] they are not interested in communication. They hate humans and think them very lowly and stupid. In any case, if you think you have one in your house, don't ever think you can challenge it. It would just love to show off to you how weak you really are.[15]

Demons can be cast out of a place through religious exorcisms or simply through strong commands to leave. Other tactics include sprinkling the home with herbs such as sandalwood or bay leaves believed to ward off evil. Some Wiccan witches also say they can perform magical spells to end demon hauntings.

"Riddles of Significance"

I t is often said that when phantoms appear they are wearing clothing from a bygone era. However, as nineteenth-century satirist Ambrose Bierce writes in *Devil's Dictionary*, it would seem that the appearance of ghostly clothing could be used to disprove the entire belief in apparitions:

> There is one [insurmountable] obstacle to a belief in ghosts. A ghost never comes naked: he appears either in a winding-sheet [a sheet that a corpse is wrapped in before burial] or [as believers say] "in his habit as he

The Smurl Demon

One of the most bizarre examples of a demon haunting took place between 1974 and 1987 in a home that was inhabited by Jack and Janet Smurl and their four daughters, twins Shannon and Carin and their older teenaged sisters, Dawn and Heather. The Smurls lived." To believe in him, then, is to believe that not only have the dead the power to make themselves visible after there is nothing left of them, but that the same power [exists] in textile fabrics. Supposing the products of the loom to have this ability, what object would they have in exercising it? And why does not the apparition of a suit of clothes sometimes walk abroad without a ghost in it? These be riddles of significance. They reach away down and get a convulsive grip on the very tap-root of this flourishing faith.

Ambrose Bierce, *The Devil's Dictionary*, Curmudgeony Librarian, 2003. www.geocities.com.

moved into the duplex, built in the late nineteenth century in West Pittston, Pennsylvania, in 1974, and peculiar events began taking place almost immediately. An unplugged television burst into flames, new water pipes leaked and broke for no apparent reason, and, most frighteningly, deep claw marks, like those of a wild animal, were found on a new sink and bathtub in a freshly remodeled bathroom. By 1977 the Smurls were convinced their house was haunted, but by a benevolent, if annoying, ghost. Toilets flushed by themselves, footsteps could be heard throughout the house at all hours, and disgusting smells suddenly wafted into rooms. As a large family of modest means, the Smurls could not afford to move.

In 1985 the hauntings intensified, and it soon became apparent that a demon, not a ghost, was haunting the house. This was at first signaled by the sounds of pigs grunting and squealing inside the walls. This is a sign that ghost investigators, or parapsychologists, associate with the presence of demons. The hog sounds were followed by a menacing voice shouting loud, obscene threats at family members. Janet soon saw the suspected source of the voice when a dark, faceless, humanlike entity appeared in the kitchen and then dematerialized by walking through the wall. After that, the activity increased in frequency and intensity. The night before Heather was about to be confirmed into the Catholic religion on the occasion of her thirteenth birthday, a large ceiling fan crashed to the floor near Shannon, almost killing her. The demon soon began throwing family members about. Shannon was pulled from bed and tossed down the stairs with the family German shepherd while Janet was plucked from bed and thrown across the room. Sometimes commotion such as scratching, grunting, and screaming inside the walls was so loud the neighbors could hear it.

In 1986 the Smurls contacted Ed and Lorraine Warren, psychical researchers from Connecticut. The Warrens visited the haunted home with a psychic named Rosemary Frueh and determined that the house contained a demon that was probably inactive for years

but was awakened by the emotional energy of the teenage girls who lived in the house. The Warrens tried to drive off the demon by playing tapes of loud religious music for hours at a time. This caused the spirit to react violently, shaking furniture and warning the Warrens to leave the house immediately. Ed Warren was choked by an invisible force and fell ill with a bad case of the flu. Carin was next to get sick, suffering from a fever that nearly killed her.

A priest was brought in to recite the mass in Latin and perform ancient exorcism rites. A medium was also contacted, and after performing a séance, she determined that the Smurl home was inhabited by four spirits: three ghosts and a demon.

By August 1986 the Smurl case was attracting national attention after a newspaper story appeared in the *Wilkes-Barre Sunday Independent* newspaper. The Smurls appeared on a local television interview show, and a book, *The Haunted*, was written about the case. Finally exhausted and discouraged by the entire affair, the Smurls moved to another town. In 1988 the Scranton Catholic diocese oversaw another exorcism in the house. This time it appeared to work; the demon seemed to disappear, and the house remains quiet. In 1991 the movie *The Haunted* was made about the case.

While skeptics question the existence of haunted houses filled with demons, poltergeists, and ghosts, no one could convince the Smurl or Estes families that they were not real. Whether the horror is caused by spirits of the dead, nonhuman entities from hell, or manifestations from overactive imaginations, it matters little to the terrified victims. For these people, the world is a haunted place, and their homes are not safe refuges from the world outside but rather are the playgrounds of wicked spirits from the other side.

CHAPTER 2

Real Haunted Houses

There are many types of haunted houses in the world. They are found in isolated rural areas, urban metropolises, and nondescript suburbs. Whether the homes belong to kings, peasants, or middle-class families, they all have one thing in common. Spirits of those who once lived there have not completely left the building. In most cases these ghosts experienced some sort of problem in their last living moments that prevented them from crossing over to the dimension of the dead.

Most often the spirits that haunt houses did not die of natural causes. They may have been murdered, committed suicide, or died by some accident such as drowning in the bathtub, electrocution, or a tumble down the stairs. The bad energy from such experiences is said to remain in the house where the unnatural death took place. In the years and centuries that follow, the specters continue to return to the residence where they experienced significant events during their living hours and dying moments. They reveal themselves by opening doors, walking about, and appearing in three-dimensional space before disappearing into thin air.

Movies and television shows often portray haunted houses as boarded up, decrepit houses with loose shutters, peeling paint, and weedy yards. But spirit-inhabited homes can be anything from utterly unremarkable two-bedroom bungalows to country cottages, tiny apartments, or magnificent castles. In fact, the only thing a residence needs to qualify as haunted, according to Holzer, "is the *presence* of an earthbound spirit, a ghost, unable to break free of the emotional turmoil of his or her physical passing."[16] And contrary to media stereotypes, these spirits are usually harmless, and the houses they haunt are safe to live in. Ironically, it is only when so-called ghost hunters are called in to drive the spirit from its residence that the houses become scenes of chaos, confusion, and danger. Perhaps this is understandable because few entities, living or dead, like to get evicted. In some cases, however, the spirit will leave willingly if the mortals who share its home will perform a few necessary tasks so that the wandering dead can finally rest in peace.

Emaciated and Squalid

A story about a ghost requiring help from the living provides one of the earliest descriptions of a haunted house. The tale was first recorded in the letters of Pliny the Younger, a philosopher and author from ancient Rome. Writing around the first century A.D., Pliny tells of a large, roomy house in Athens, Greece, where residents heard iron clashing and chains rattling in the dead of night. The sounds would seem to be off in the distance when

Haunted houses are found in isolated rural areas, urban metropolises, and nondescript suburbs.

they began but would soon draw near. The nerve-wracking noises served notice to residents that a ghost was about to appear, as Pliny writes, "in the form of an old man, of extremely emaciated and squalid appearance, with a long beard and disheveled hair, rattling the chains on his feet and hands."[17] This occurrence caused the distraught occupants to lie awake at night in fear. Some family members became ill from the experience; others died. As a result, the house was abandoned to the apparition.

While few new tenants could be found to lease the property, not everyone was afraid. When the philosopher Athenodorus heard about the haunted dwelling, he was eager to rent it so that he could confront the apparition. The first night in the house Athenodorus decided to stay awake and wait for the old man to appear. To distract himself, he wrote philosophical texts with his pencil and tablet. Around 3:00 AM, the distant sound of chains was heard, growing louder until the specter was soon standing nearby. With a beckoning finger, the ghost implored Athenodorus to follow it outside to the garden. The philosopher did as he was told, but the apparition quickly vanished once outdoors. However, Athenodorus made a mark in the grass where the thing had disappeared. Pliny picks up the story:

> The next day [Athenodorus] gave information to the magistrates, and advised them to order that spot to be dug up. This was accordingly done, and the skeleton of a man in chains was found there; for the body, having lain a considerable time in the ground, was putrefied and moldered away from the fetters. The bones, being collected together, were publicly buried, and thus after the ghost was

A first-century story about a ghost requiring help from the living provides one of the earliest descriptions of a haunted house.

appeased by the proper ceremonies, the house was haunted no more.[18]

"Fetch Poor Dickie Back"

Stories of apparitions materializing numerous times to tell the living that they want to be properly buried are common. In a few cases, however, the spirit of the dead one wishes to instead remain among the living. Such is the case of Dickie, a skull that resides in a farmhouse in Derbyshire, England. The apparition that thrives within the skull performs beneficial services to the living in order to stay in favor with the home's occupants.

Dickie has been haunting the rural Tunstead Farm for nearly 400 years, sitting on its favorite spot in the house, a sunny windowsill. Throughout the centuries, more than 50 different residents have reported that Dickie will open doors for them if their arms are full or wake servants who oversleep in the morning. Most of the time the specter remains peaceful and inconspicuous but will make rattling noises or tap on the window if animals in the barn are ill or about to give birth. On one occasion, when a suspicious stranger approached Tunstead Farm, the skull specter made thudding noises that shook the entire house. This awakened the family, who quickly gave chase to a burglar about to break into their home.

Woe will befall any who remove Dickie from his windowsill. In past centuries, on separate occasions, Dickie was thrown into a local river, buried in a church cemetery, and stolen by thieves. In the first incident, the barn roof collapsed, nearly killing the resident farmer. The second time, livestock died, crops failed, and mysterious storms created havoc. And the thieves who stole Dickey made the mistake of taking the skull to the nearby village

The Most Actively Haunted Mansion

The Whaley House in San Diego is a two-story mansion built in 1857 and the oldest brick structure in Southern California. According to *Hans Holzer's Travel Guide to Haunted Houses*, the Whaley House is also one of the most haunted houses in the world:

> Numerous witnesses . . . have seen ghosts here. Manifestations include the figure of a woman . . . sounds of footsteps; upstairs windows opening by themselves despite strong bolts installed so they could be opened only from inside; a man in a frock coat and pantaloons at the top of the stairs; organ music . . . [in a room] where there is an organ—though at the time no one was near it and the cover closed; even a ghost dog scurrying down the hall toward the dining room. A black

rocking chair upstairs moves of its own volition at times, as if someone were sitting in it. A woman in a green plaid gingham dress has been seated in one of the

The Whaley House, in San Diego, California, is thought to be one of the most haunted houses in the world.

bedrooms upstairs. People have smelled perfume and cigars. A child ghost has been observed by people working in the house and a baby has been heard crying. Strange lights, cool breezes and cold spots add to the general atmosphere of haunting. Whaley House is probably one of the most actively haunted mansions in the world today.

Hans Holzer, *Han Holzer's Travel Guide to Haunted Houses*. New York: Black Dog & Leventhal, 1998, p. 27.

of Disley. According to historian J. Castle Hall, upon Dickie's arrival a moaning voice was heard in every house in the village. It said, "Fetch poor Dickie back. . . . Fetch poor Dickie back. . . ."[19] The skull was promptly returned to the farm, where it remains today.

Although Dickie has made Tunstead Farm a well-known haunted house, the specter's origins remain something of a mystery. Some believe it is the skull of Ned Dickson, who originally owned the farm but left home to fight as a mercenary soldier in the late 1580s. When Dickson failed to return after nine years, his cousin assumed he was dead, took control of Tunstead Farm, and married his wife. Dickson came home in 1590, and although he was badly injured, he attempted to reclaim his property and his spouse. Instead, he was murdered by the newlyweds and buried on the grounds. After that time, the couple's life was fraught with bad luck. They consulted a witch, who told them to unearth Dickson's skull and place it in their home. After this was done, their fortunes improved, and although the dead soldier continued to haunt their house, he looked over the affairs of the subsequent residents.

This story is disputed by those who say Dickie's spirit is that of a young woman named Dickson who was murdered at the farm. As she lay dying, she commanded that her bones never leave the place she loved so well. Since that time, while her skull remains on the windowsill, a female wraith haunts the farm, floating through the kitchen on occasion before disappearing into a wall.

Whether Dickie is male or female, the ghost has literally changed the course of local history. In the 1850s the London and North Western Railway Company wanted to build a railroad through the lands occupied by Tunstead Farm. The owners were legally obligated to sell the right-of-way across their property to the railway company. However, when construction began on Tunstead Farm, a series of mysterious landslides and work accidents plagued the project. Unable to complete the link, the rail line was diverted to another parcel of land. Although engineers attributed the problem to unstable ground, local residents gave credit to Dickie for saving Tunstead Farm. Today a nearby bridge on the line is named for Dickie, a grinning skull that guards Tunstead Farm and drives away those who would bring harm to the property.

Britain's Most Haunted Castle

Although Dickie lives in a humble farmhouse, many of England's most famous ghosts reside in castles built hundreds of years ago. These former fortresses are places where battles were fought, lust and greed claimed many a royal life, and where hundreds died hideously in torture chambers. Most castles are said to house long-dead ghosts of kings and queens, servants and soldiers. They are said to walk the halls, gallop through the grounds, and pop up in bedrooms at regular intervals.

One of the most haunted houses in Great Britain, Windsor Castle, is also the most famous. Built by William the Conqueror in Berkshire County in 1070, Windsor is the oldest castle in the world to be continuously occupied by a royal family. And with a floor area of 484,000 square feet (44,944 sq m.), about the size of 250 average homes, there has always been plenty of room for ghosts to roam. The list of ghosts said to be living in Windsor Castle is almost as long as the list of royals who have lived there. One of the most famous residents, King Henry VIII, who acceded to the throne in 1509, has been seen on several occasions limping through the halls of Windsor, moaning in agony with each

The list of ghosts said to be living in Windsor Castle is almost as long as the list of royals who have resided there. One of the most famous residents, King Henry VIII, who acceded to the throne in 1509, has been seen on several occasions limping through the halls of Windsor, moaning in agony with each footstep.

footstep. Perhaps this ghost is still suffering from a thigh wound Henry obtained during a jousting match in 1536. The ulcerated wound is said to have led to the king's death in 1547.

Henry VIII is famous for having had six wives and several mistresses, but the treatment of his second wife, Anne Boleyn, has allegedly had a lasting effect on residents of Windsor. Boleyn married Henry in 1533, but their relationship soured when Anne gave birth to a daughter before having several miscarriages. Unhappy that Anne could not produce a son to be his heir, Henry had her arrested, saying she had used witchcraft to entrap him in marriage. He also accused her of adultery, incest with her brother, and treason for conspiring to kill him. Even though the charges were false, and the case was presided over by Anne's uncle, the queen was beheaded in May 1536. Since that time, her ghost has been seen dozens of times standing at the window in the castle's monastery.

Haunted castle ruins like these in northern England are said to be teeming with the ghosts of those who were killed in battle or executed for political reasons.

King George III, who reigned from 1760 to 1820, was also known to suffer from depression and madness. During long spells of lunacy, Mad King George, as he was known, would talk nonstop for up to 58 hours, claiming to converse with the angels. At such times, George was locked away in the Royal Library. Since his

King Henry VIII's second wife, Anne Boleyn, center, was executed after Henry deemed her an unfit wife. Her ghost has been haunting Windsor Castle since her beheading in 1536.

death, the ghost of the mad king has been reportedly seen wandering around the bookshelves or staring out the windows.

Other famous ghosts of Windsor include Queen Elizabeth I, who died in 1603, and King Charles I, who was beheaded during the English Revolution in 1649. Windsor is also purportedly home to a horned demon with the head of a stag that is said to bring disease or death to anyone who sees it. Few have reported the presence of this spirit, however, perhaps because of the ghost of Herne the Hunter. In the fourteenth century, Herne saved King Richard II from being mauled by a cornered stag. Since his death, Herne's spirit is said to roam Windsor Woods searching for souls and hunting hellish demons.

Screaming Bloody Murder

There are few ghosts in the United States that can be traced to royalty. However, there are hundreds of uniquely American apparitions in the United States that may be found haunting houses and reenacting historical horrors. Several of these ghosts may be traced to the nineteenth century, when slavery was legal and slaves often died under the most violent of circumstances. It is said that the ghosts of these slaves remained behind to remind future generations of their pain and misery. One such spirit is Luther, a runaway slave who escaped from a cotton plantation in Alabama in 1857 and made his way north through the Underground Railroad, a series of safe houses in which slaves were hidden by sympathetic citizens. One of the stops on the Underground Railroad was the old Millfield Inn, located about 10 miles (16km) east of Athens, Ohio. Built in 1811, the inn was a large home constructed on a foundation of ancient hickory and ash trees. A giant stone chimney runs up the center of the place and

The ghost of an escaped slave named Luther is said to haunt the Millfield Inn near Athens, Ohio. Luther died in the attic of the home in 1850.

provides heat for each of the 10 rooms. In the attic, behind the chimney and under the floorboards, a secret room was built to hide slaves like Luther as they made their way north to Canada, where they would find freedom.

The Millfield Inn was a private residence in 1850 when Luther arrived at the door in bad shape. On the run from slave hunters, Luther had taken a bullet in the thigh. Limping and bleeding for days through the muddy paths of southern Ohio, Luther's wound was infected and gangrenous by the time he was given a hot meal and a warm place to sleep in the secret attic room. Luther died, but in his last hours he was driven mad by pain and anger. When his time came, he did not rest in peace. Several days later Luther was seen staggering through a cornfield behind the inn, dressed in rags, and carrying the bloody stump of his shot-up leg. In the years that followed, Luther would occasionally appear in the secret room or on the porch of the Millfield Inn, screaming bloody murder by the light of the moon.

Haunted New Orleans

Another gruesome story concerning secret rooms and slave hauntings comes from New Orleans, where the Royal Street residence of Delphine and Louis LaLaurie sits among the splendid homes in the city's renowned French Quarter. The LaLauries moved into the house in 1832, and it quickly became a center for grand parties among the city's most respected citizens. However, the fine china, expensive wine, and tasteful French furniture hid a dark secret. Madame LaLaurie owned many slaves and treated them in a brutal manner. In one incident, Delphine was seen wielding an 8-foot-long (2.4m) bullwhip and chasing a young slave girl onto the roof of the house. To escape the thrashings of the enraged mistress, the girl jumped to her death.

Although the LaLauries remained popular with the New Orleans gentry, in 1834 the façade of gentility was ripped away from their fabulous home. A fire was reported by one of the neighbors, and when volunteer firemen arrived, they discovered a huge hidden room in the attic. Dozens of slaves were chained to walls or were living in cages. Some had been gruesomely mutilated in what seemed to be grisly medical experiments. Various severed limbs and skulls lay strewn about the floor.

Even in a region where slavery was legal, few could comprehend Madame LaLaurie's brutality. Calls quickly went out for the high-society matron to be put on trial for her despicable behavior. Before she could be arrested, however, Delphine LaLaurie disappeared. Some say she went to France, others say she moved out to the rural Louisiana countryside. Whatever the case, neighbors trashed the house, destroying its elegant furnishings and tearing out the walls of the room where the slaves had been tortured.

The Ghosts of Slavery's Past

The LaLaurie house was abandoned, and the doors and windows were covered with boards for more than 40 years. Eventually, however, the home was used for various purposes, but the ghosts of slavery's past remained within its walls. It is said the ghosts approved of the all-girl high school that occupied the home from 1865 until 1880. However, they hated the music conservatory that moved in the following year. On the night of a planned concert, no one showed up, so the owner closed the school. It is said that the spirits held a wild party the next night, and riotous ghost music was heard echoing throughout the neighborhood.

For a time the premises were used as a boarding house, and residents claimed to have seen the phantom slave girl running across the roof, chased by the whip-wielding LaLaurie. At the beginning of the twentieth century, one of the poor immigrants living in the house saw a black man lugging chains up the stairs. When the boarder tried to intervene, the ghost allegedly attacked him before disappearing. In 1942 a bar called The Haunted Saloon, opened in one of the downstairs rooms. The barkeep kept a notebook of the hauntings experienced by his not-so-sober patrons. However, few local residents were willing to patronize a bar with such a violent past, and the building was again abandoned. Eventually a furniture store moved to the location, but, like the bar, it had a hard time attracting customers. This might be attributed to the unidentifiable, foul-smelling, mucuslike green slime that occasionally was found to cover the merchandise.

Between 1969 and 2005 the LaLaurie house served as an apartment building with 20 units. It was purchased by a physician who restored it to its former magnificence. In April 2007 actor Nicolas Cage bought the mansion. While no ghosts have been seen in the past several decades, the LaLaurie house is still considered to be one of the most haunted houses in New Orleans.

Famous Haunted Houses

The crimes of Madame LaLaurie sound as if they were taken from a horror story written by nineteenth-century author Edgar Allan Poe. His classic tales of the macabre feature hidden rooms, ghosts, and tortured souls in chains. Poe often wrote about the spirit world, and in the 1844 story "The Premature Burial," he describes the unearthly realm where ghosts are said to exist: "The boundaries which divide Life from Death are at best shadowy and vague. Who shall say where the one ends, and where the other begins?"[20]

Poe was only 39 when he died in 1849, and his last hours were spent trembling and hallucinating in a state of madness. His death was blamed on opium, alcohol, and possibly rabies. Few who understand the circumstances surrounding the horror writer's death are surprised to learn that his house is haunted. However, Poe did not die in his little four-room Baltimore home, built in 1830, but at a nearby hospital. Poe's grandmother did die in the house in 1835, and it may be her spirit that is wandering about the Poe House, which is today a museum.

Many other people have lived and died in the Poe abode, but whatever is haunting the house was not seen until 1968, during the riots that followed the death of civil rights activist Martin Luther King Jr. At that time of civil unrest and violence, police were called to the Poe House because they saw lights flickering on and off in several rooms, beginning on the first floor, moving to the second floor, and remaining in the garret. Believing that rioters had broken in and were about to set it on fire, police surrounded the museum. However, since no one had a key, authorities did not enter the building. Guards watched the doors all night long, and in the morning they entered the building when the curator arrived with a key. No one and nothing could be found.

Following the incident of the mysterious lights, several visitors to the museum were tapped on the shoulder when they were alone in the grandmother's bedroom. The curator, named Jerome, commented on these incidents: "This happened over a period of months, and the people were tourists, from all over the country, so it's not likely to be some sort of conspiracy."[21]

Perhaps the most dramatic incident occurred in 1985, when a theater group was getting ready to perform Poe's play *Bernice* at the house where it was written. An actress was preparing in a back room once inhabited by Poe's wife, Virginia, when a window fell out of its frame and crashed to the floor. The shutters had been closed on the outside, so there was no chance that wind caused the incident. According to Jerome, "Someone would have had to physically pull it up out of the grooves it was resting in and then drop it on the floor. Psychics have told me it was a spirit just making its presence known. I don't think the actress could have done it, because it really shook her up. She gave a bad performance; after that, she was that shaken."[22]

On other occasions, the curator found doors and windows flung open. And although the surrounding neighborhood is full of drug dealers and gang members, the Poe House has never been a site of criminal activity. According to a 1985 story in the *New York Times*, street gangs do not enter the house for fear of ghosts.

The Haunted White House

Located not far from Baltimore, the city of Washington, D.C., is home to the most famous house in the world, the White House. Home to U.S. presidents since 1800, the White House is also said to be one of the most haunted homes in America. From the basement bowling alley to the bedrooms where presidents sleep, White House residents and visitors have heard disembodied footsteps, ghostly knocking, laughter of the dead, and music from the world beyond.

The Yellow Oval Room on the second-floor residence was first

Presidents John Adams, Andrew Jackson, and Abraham Lincoln are said to haunt the White House in Washington, D.C.

Haunted Houses

occupied by president John Adams and his wife, Abigail, in 1801. On several occasions, Abigail's apparition has been seen walking through the hallway, arms outstretched as if carrying something. And although Thomas Jefferson never lived in the White House, he has been heard playing his fiddle in the Yellow Oval Room on hot summer nights when the moon is full.

The seventh president, Andrew Jackson, did live in the White House but apparently never left. Although he died in 1845, his ghost was seen swearing, cursing, and stomping through the Queen's Bedroom in 1862 by Mary Todd Lincoln, wife of Abraham Lincoln.

The ghost of President Lincoln has also visited the White House on many occasions. Some say he is trying to finish his second term, which was cut short by an assassin's bullet. One of the earliest sightings was reported in 1889, when a bodyguard for president Benjamin Harrison was continually disturbed late at night by unexplainable footsteps in a hall. The bodyguard grew so tired of jumping into action to defend Harrison that he organized a séance to beg Lincoln to stop haunting the halls so he could get some sleep.

Lincoln also allegedly appears at times of national crisis, striding up and down the second-floor hallway, rapping at doors, and standing in windows with his hands clasped behind his back. This may have been the reason Lincoln appeared in 1941, months before the United States entered World War II. At the time, Lincoln's ghost awakened Queen Wilhelmina of the Netherlands by knocking on the door of the Lincoln Bedroom (a room that Lincoln never slept in but that contains his bed). When Wilhelmina opened the door, the sixteenth president was standing there. The queen fainted, and when she awoke Lincoln's ghost remained,

Did You Know?

The White House basement is said to be haunted by a black cat. It is regarded as an omen of bad luck.

looking over her. The next day, the queen told president Franklin Roosevelt about Lincoln's appearance. Roosevelt stated that he too had seen the president's phantom on several occasions and that the spirit of Lincoln would doubtlessly wander the White House halls forever.

Not all White House ghosts are presidents and first ladies. One of the most dreaded phantoms is a black cat that haunts the basement. Regarded as an omen of bad luck, the ghost cat has been seen by White House staff before national tragedies, including the stock market crash of 1929 and the assassination of president John F. Kennedy in 1963.

There are thousands of haunted houses throughout the world. Tales of their troubled pasts have inspired books, movies, and countless television shows. Whether the stories are true remains unknown. One thing that can be certain, however: like the ghosts themselves, the spooky tales will continue to terrify the living and undoubtedly take on a life of their own for centuries to come.

CHAPTER 3

Nasty, Noisy, Horrific Hauntings

Many houses inhabited by ghosts can be creepy or terrifying, but most apparitions are actually harmless. However, it is said that about 2 percent of all hauntings are caused not by innocuous ghosts but by harmful or downright deadly poltergeists. Unlike ghosts, these apparitions can cause knives or heavy furniture to fly through the air, make bricks fall from walls, or perform other nasty feats that can break limbs, crush skulls, and squash torsos. Poltergeists are also known to cause great harm through fire and water, as Joseph Braddock writes in *Haunted Houses of Great Britain*:

> They are often incendiaries, fire-raisers; and, apparently, through the agency of these too commonly supposed harmless ghosts, scores of people have been badly burnt. Lighted matches have fallen

from ceilings; mattresses have started to smoke and smolder; and in 1929 at Lillington Avenue, Leamington, [in central England] during other poltergeist disturbances, a saucepan of *cold* water, containing peeled potatoes, began to boil over at midnight, when there was no fire in the kitchen range on which the saucepan rested.[23]

These events can cause physical harm and extreme mental stress. Victims may suffer from neurosis, depression, chronic anxiety, or even post-traumatic stress disorder, a condition common to soldiers who have been through battle. While such cases are rare, they are well documented and have become part of haunted-house lore.

Poltergeists can be so virulent that renowned ghost hunter Harry Price says, "While a ghost *haunts*, a poltergeist *Infests*."[24] For example, when compared to other ghosts that tend to remain hidden and prefer solitude, poltergeists appear to enjoy being an annoyance. They seem nearly impossible to permanently evict from a household. And whereas ghosts generally do their haunting at night, poltergeists like to harass people during the day.

Torments in Texas

The Beaird family of Tyler, Texas, was unfortunate enough to experience life with a nasty poltergeist firsthand. Between 1964 and 1968, Howard and his wife, Johnnie, and their son, Andy, suffered one awful experience after another. This poltergeist committed many ugly acts with bugs, slugs, fire, and flying objects.

In most poltergeist hauntings, the spirit is said to feed off the energy of one of the victims, called an agent, who involuntarily and unknowingly fuels the demonic deeds. In the Beaird case, the poltergeist may have been drawing energy from two family members, 13-year-old Andy and Johnnie, who was only living in the house part time. The Beaird's ghastly troubles began almost immediately after they moved into the house. Both Howard and Johnnie had recently retired after working together for decades at the same company. Howard started a small rubber-stamp business in the garage, but Johnnie's behavior became erratic upon her retirement. She stopped cooking and cleaning and became introverted, walking to restaurants in Tyler and dining alone every day. She also claimed that people were spying on her. When Howard disputed this claim, Johnnie accused him of being in charge of the spies, claiming he had hidden television cameras in the house to observe her behavior. Johnnie also took up tobacco for the first time at the age of 60, chain-smoking cigarettes and cigars and using snuff. Although there were many ashtrays throughout the house, she began laying down her cigarettes and cigars in a careless fashion, leaving burn marks on furniture and making holes in the mattress.

Both Andy and Howard were extremely troubled by Johnnie's behavior, but they soon realized they had additional problems. One night in July 1965, their home was suddenly infested with hundreds of large June bugs, even though the windows were closed. As Howard told Hans Holzer in a detailed letter:

> Andy and I would go to bed, and as soon as we turned out the light we were plagued by hordes of June bugs of all sizes, which would hit us on our heads and faces, some glancing off on the floor, others landing on the bed, and some missing us

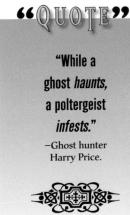

The Beaird family, of Texas, were allegedly attacked by hoards of June bugs every time they turned out their lights. The attacks would stop abruptly as soon as the lights were turned on, and the bugs would lie dead on the floor.

entirely and smashing themselves against the metal window blinds. Night after night we fought these bugs in the dark, grabbing those that landed on the bed and throwing them against the blinds as hard as we could. Then we discovered that at least half of the bugs that hit us were *already dead*, in fact had been dead so long that they were crisp and would crumble between our fingers when we picked them up![25]

When Howard turned on the lights, the raids stopped and no bugs could be seen in the air, but hundreds of June bug corpses were piled on the floor. If the lights were then turned off, the attacks resumed, even after Howard and Andy stuffed rags in the cracks of the doors.

Flying Slugs and Disembodied Voices

Soon other events commenced that are commonly associated with the fiery aspects of poltergeist activity. One night, during the hottest part of the summer, Howard found the wall heater in the bathroom turned on as high as possible, causing flames to flicker onto the wall above. He turned off the gas and, suspecting Johnnie of causing the incident, removed the handle so that it could not be turned on. However, the heater continued to light by itself. On one occasion, Howard smelled smoke and rushed into the bathroom to find the heater running full blast, burning paper towels that someone—or something— had stuffed into the burners. Johnnie denied starting the fire and blamed Howard or Andy for starting the blaze. Despite her denials, Howard thought it best to get Johnnie out of the house, and she soon moved in with her sister-in-law, who lived in Daingerfield, Texas, about 100 miles (161km) from Tyler.

To be sure his wife was not sneaking into the house, Howard changed the locks on all of the doors. Johnnie's form appeared several times, however, as a ghost in the backyard or simply as a hand hovering by Howard's head. Upon these occasions, Howard called Daingerfield to confirm that Johnnie was with her sister-in-law. The poltergeist activity increased. While lying in bed one night, Howard heard a disembodied voice that, although it did not sound like Johnnie, began telling stories from the early years of their marriage that only she would know. In the weeks that followed, at least six other voices seemed to be haunting the house, emerging out of thin air and carrying on conversations with Howard. Many of the voices could be traced to family acquaintances, including people who had been dead for years. The voice of one man was particularly spooky. Several days after his

Once the June bug attacks stopped, more furious attacks by slugs began on the Beaird family. Howard Beaird claims the slugs hit the family with such force it seemed they were being fired from a gun.

voice was heard echoing throughout the house, he died in a car accident.

Meanwhile, the bug raids continued but became even more disgusting when the June bugs were replaced by 3-inch-long

(8cm) slugs as fat as cocktail wieners. Although slugs do not fly, Howard claims that they hit him and Andy as if they were shot out of a gun. Other types of bugs, such as pill bugs and wood lice, also became part of the bug attacks, along with dangerous objects such as carpenter nails and large chunks of rock salt.

More typical poltergeist activity ensued when things such as shoes, wallets, gloves, lit cigars, furniture, and other objects began to fly through the air, often hitting or narrowly missing Howard or Andy. Bed sheets were violently pulled off the bed and the occupants thrown heavily to the floor. The poltergeist also made disgusting piles of filth appear in Johnnie's bed. These consisted of mud mixed with broken pieces of soap, old hair, and burned matches. The first time this happened, the mess was accompanied by a note, written in a young child's scrawl, that said, "Evil spirits go away."[26]

This note signaled the beginning of a long-running correspondence between the spirit world and the Beairds as notes and letters began to mysteriously appear on a regular basis. Many were in Johnnie's handwriting although she was residing in another town. The notes seemed to predict the future. They listed the names of friends and relatives next to the years they were born and dates sometime in the future, apparently when they would die. One note even mentioned Johnnie, which read, "Death 1991."[27]

"Bill Is NUTTY"

Month after month, Howard and Andy dealt with the nightmare of living in a house haunted by poltergeists. Masses of bugs, living and dead, large and small, continued to inundate them night after night. If the lights were left on, the attacks were carried out

by invisible insects that could be felt but not seen. While some events were dangerous, such as the fires, others were humorous. For example, Andy found a check with the "pay to" line made out to a brand of whiskey, reading, "Johnny Walker, $1,000,000." The "for" line was addressed to an unknown person, reading, "Bill is NUTTY," and the signature line read "ha ha."[28]

By December 1965, Howard and Andy were being bombarded with 10 to 15 notes every day that materialized out of thin air, folded themselves before their eyes, and either fell to the floor or hit them. Some were written by family acquaintances both living and dead. Other notes were from people unknown to the Beairds or from public figures such as Marilyn Monroe, who died in 1961. The handwriting often seemed to be a disjointed style similar to Johnnie's or Andy's. Several of the ghostly writers made repeat visits, such as a Mrs. Elliot, a friend who had been dead for several years, and a Mr. Gree, who was unknown to the family. The notes, while discussing other spirits, family members, and the events that were taking place in the Beaird household, were conversational in tone and read like personal letters that close friends might write. For example, Mrs. Elliot often worried about Andy and real or imagined conflicts between the teenager and his parents. Mrs. Elliot wrote a rather disturbing missive about taking Andy, whom she called "Junior," into the spirit world where she could care for him:

> Howard, I need to write you notes. Junior has had to worry so much. Why do you mind him coming with me? He would be happy. It would be right for him not to worry. I agree he must get an education but at seventeen he could get a course

and get into college. In the meantime I will help John [Johnnie] and him. He could play music and he would be great at seventeen. He would also like to take care of the house. John would get so much better. You would be better financially and Junior could get better. . . . You had better pay attention because he wants to come. I have all the divine right to take him.[29]

Mrs. Elliot and Mr. Gree also communicated with disembodied voices that could be heard throughout the house. On one occasion, Mr. Gree used the kitchen telephone, moving the rotary dial with invisible fingers and speaking into the mouthpiece as it hovered in the air. The conversation was apparently private, as the spirit asked Howard and Andy to leave the room while it was talking.

The Work of the Devil?

In February 1967 Johnnie moved back into the Elizabeth Street house, but the hauntings did not seem to bother her. Andy, however, was showing signs of stress. As a child he was known for his gregarious personality and sense of humor, but as a teenager he had become shy and introverted.

With Johnnie's return, the poltergeist activity moved to another level. Large, heavy objects moved about the house. A huge chest of drawers was found teetering precipitously in the middle of Howard's bed. The refrigerator was moved to a bedroom, although there were no marks in the carpeting to indicate that anyone had dragged it across the house. Most bizarre, on several occasions the large dining table was found in the attic, which had a door opening that measured only 16 by 24 inches (41 by 61cm).

Scared Stiff of Ghosts

Sometimes alleged cases of poltergeist hauntings are outright fraud committed by people who wish to draw attention to themselves. At other times, the motive can be to frighten family members, as Michael Clarkson writes in *Poltergeists*:

> [An] elderly man [in a] Victorian house was said to have loud, poltergeist-type noises that had driven away his son, daughter-in-law, and grandchild. After investigating, [a parapsychologist] discovered the man had rigged an ingenious device in which he created the peculiar noises. At night with his relatives in bed, the man would pull on a wire at

After this impossible deed, the table would return to its proper place in the dining room.

In April 1968 the Beairds finally had enough. They left their house of horrors on Elizabeth Street, never to return. After the move, Johnnie stopped smoking and the family was not bothered the side of a downstairs fireplace, setting off a noisy contraption hidden under floorboards, which consisted of two tin mugs, an iron bar, and a biscuit tin with two wooden balls in it. When the wire was pulled, it started the noises which became amplified in two upstairs bedrooms.

It turned out his motivation was not to get attention from authorities or the media, but to be rid of his kin. "Well, mate," he told [the parapsychologist], "you don't know my daughter-in-law. . . . I was in the way and she was trying to make it seem that I was funny in the head and ought to be in an old people's home. Well, I knew what to do. She was scared stiff of ghosts."

Michael Clarkson, *Poltergeists*. Buffalo, NY: Firefly, 2005, p. 40.

by any further poltergeist incidents.

There is little research available to explain the long-running and numerous peculiarities experienced by the Beairds, but Holzer used his knowledge of parapsychology to provide answers to the bewildered family. It was first determined that both Andy and

Johnnie were mentally unstable individuals who emitted large reserves of uncontrolled psychic energy. After conducting a detailed analysis of the handwritten notes, Holzer concluded that they were written by either Andy or Johnnie. However, Holzer believes that the notes were not consciously written by the son or mother. Instead, "actual non-physical entities were, in fact, using the untapped energies of these two unfortunate individuals to express themselves in the physical world."[30] This energy, according to believers, can also dematerialize objects and rematerialize them in different places. This would explain the notes falling out of the air or the refrigerator landing in a bedroom. Whatever the explanation, after the Beairds left, the next owners of the house also noticed odd noises and occasional movements of furniture. However, the new residents apparently did not have mentally unstable family members to draw poltergeists out of the spirit world. In addition, members of the second family were deeply religious and did not believe in supernatural phenomena such as poltergeists. They would barely discuss the issue with Holzer, telling him it was all the work of the devil.

Electricity and Magnetism?

While demons are often blamed for horrific hauntings, there may be scientific explanations for some poltergeist activity. For example, some areas of the planet have unusual magnetic or electrical properties that could theoretically cause objects to float in the air or cause problems with electricity. This might have been the case in a 2003 occurrence at a home in Leawood, Kansas, where doorknobs jiggled, cold spots appeared and disappeared, and electrical appliances either turned on spontaneously or operated without being plugged into a wall socket. Researchers with electromagnetic-field detectors discovered that a geomagnetic field, like a weak version of the magnetic North Pole, was located near the house. Similar phenomena have been associated with homes located near high-voltage transmission towers, microwave towers, or powerful radar installations such as those used by the military. And, according to parapsychologists, when the powerful electromagnetic charges are combined with the mental energies of poltergeist agents, odd phenomena can occur. This power might even suspend gravity, and in such cases slugs could be drawn up from the ground or June bugs pulled from their flight paths to the source of the energy. How these bugs might travel through walls into a closed room, as they did on Elizabeth Street, remains a mystery.

While some are dubious that gravity can be disrupted, a Canadian researcher named John Hutchinson claims to have accomplished that feat. Hutchinson filled a room with dozens of electromagnetic devices, such as Tesla coils, electrostatic machines called Van de Graff generators, radio frequency transmitters, signal generators, and other devices. After they had been operating for a time, poltergeist activities allegedly ensued. Objects lifted off tables and hovered in the air, unusual fires broke out in other rooms of the building, a mirror jumped off the wall and smashed on the floor, water began swirling in untouched containers, lights turned on and off, and metal became white-hot but did not burn the table on which it was sitting. Like poltergeist activity, these events were sporadic and unpredictable, with the machines running for days before anything might happen. Hutchinson even claims to have a video of a 19-pound (7kg) sledgehammer floating in the air. Thus far, however, the public has yet to see it.

Half of the dead at the local graveyard was said to be haunting the house of 11-year-old Janet Harper in Enfield, England.

Telekinetic Temper Tantrums

The human aspect of poltergeist hauntings involves the mental energy allegedly emitted by disturbed adolescents and mentally ill adults. Parapsychologist William G. Roll coined the term *recurrent spontaneous psychokinesis* (RSPK) to describe this energy. RSPK refers to the capacity of individuals to involuntarily affect the physical environment with their minds, creating paranormal physical effects that occur repeatedly over a period of time.

Because poltergeist activities often resemble those of an infantile, if aggressive, spoiled child, RSPK has been called a telekinetic temper tantrum that is exacerbated by problems within a household. According to parapsychologist D. Scott Rogo, "Psychological research indicates that poltergeists focus on unhappy families who tend to repress and sublimate massive amounts of their inner aggression and anger. This anger tends to build within the unconscious mind of one of the family members until it explodes, outward in the form of the poltergeist."[31]

When such poltergeists appear, they can allegedly attract local ghosts that are haunting their home or a nearby area. The disturbed individual who unwillingly attracts these apparitions can suffer like someone possessed by the devil. They may be troubled by severe headaches, insomnia, buzzing in the ears, hallucinations, and even insanity. On very rare occasions, an unfortunate victim may be possessed by several ghosts over a long period of time. This was the case with Janet Harper, an 11-year-old girl who lived in Enfield, England. Harper's haunting began in 1977 with typical poltergeist activity. Chairs moved short distances, and loud knocking noises were heard by Janet and her divorced mother, two brothers, and sister. Soon the activities became more violent, with toys and furniture flying through the air as if they were shot out of a cannon. Mysterious pools of water appeared, and Janet often reported sensations of being bitten, pinched, and slapped. On several occasions a kitchen knife hovered in the air near Janet's head and followed her around the house.

Janet's mother called in psychic investigator Guy Playfair, who recorded 400 poltergeist incidents within a few weeks. When Playfair decided to communicate with the poltergeist, asking it to remember that it was dead, Janet's bedroom erupted in violent activity, with books, clothing, and furniture flying about the room. Then Janet herself became a victim as an unseen force

picked her up and tossed her about the room like a child's toy. This activity showed that Janet was the poltergeist's main target. Paranormal researcher Colin Wilson describes the situation:

She was often thrown out of bed seven or eight times before she succeeded in getting to sleep. When she fell asleep, she twitched and moaned. . . . On one occasion . . . she went into convulsions, screamed hysterically. . . . The following night, Janet had more convulsions, and wandered around, talking aloud. "Where's Gober. He'll kill you.". . . Soon after this, Janet began producing drawings, in a state of semi-trance; one of them showed a woman with blood pouring out of her throat, with the name "Watson" written underneath. Other drawings continued this theme of blood, knives, and death.[32]

Janet soon began channeling, or acting as a human conduit, for several spirits of the dead. One foul-mouthed entity was called Joe Watson. Another, named Bill, spoke through Janet, saying he had a dog named Gober the Ghost. When asked where he came from, Bill said, "From the graveyard." When asked why he didn't go "up there," he said in a jerky voice, "I'm not in heaven, man. . . . I am Bill Haylock and . . . I am seventy-two years old and I have come here to see my family but they are not here now. . . . I want some jazz music now go and get me some or else I'll go barmy [insane]."[33]

This odd voice, which sounded like a very old man, came out of Janet's mouth one word at a time, and Bill's conversation with Playfair lasted three hours. The investigator later stated that the number of entities haunting the Harper house consisted of "half the local graveyard."[34] The haunting was blamed on Janet's adolescent energy attracting phantasms to the house. Eventually, as Janet matured, the poltergeist activity stopped and the seemingly possessed young girl went on to live a normal life.

Clammy, Rank Spittle

Although Janet Harper was beaten and threatened by the poltergeists in her house, they did not try to kill her. However, there are rare cases of poltergeist hauntings where evil entities seemingly try to commit suicide by destroying their earthly agents. One well-known case dates from the eighteenth century when Molly and Dobby Giles, two adolescent girls who lived in Bristol, England, were bitten, cut, strangled, and nearly killed. The poltergeist activity in their home was described by ghost researcher Henry Durbin in a pamphlet called "A Narrative of Some Extraordinary Things That Happened to Mr. Richard Giles's Children." Although Durbin first visited the Giles home to debunk the stories, after living with the family, he found a host of malicious spirits haunting the home and causing great torment to the innocent young girls.

The events began in December 1761 in a typical poltergeist fashion when wine glasses and cooking utensils began flying around the kitchen. On February 19 Molly and Dobby were dragged from their beds by an unseen force. When Durbin, Richard Giles, and a brawny neighbor grabbed hold of the girls, they found themselves in a tug of war with an invisible force, with the children screaming in the middle. The men were forced to let go, and Molly and Dobby were mercilessly thrown about the bedroom. The attacks only increased in violence, and at one point Durbin observed an invisible entity trying to strangle Molly. Describing the event later, he wrote, "I saw the flesh at the side of her throat pushed in, whiten as if done with fingers, though I saw none. Her face grew red and blackish presently, as if she was strangled, but without any convulsion."[35]

Soon after the strangling, the poltergeist continued with the physical torture. Both children were pinched so badly that they had fingernail marks in their flesh. In a separate incident, Molly was cut 40 times by an unseen agent. Then the biting began. According to Durbin, seven people witnessed the attack:

> We saw their arms bitten about twenty times that evening. Their arms were put out of bed, and they lay on their backs. They could not do it themselves, as we were looking at them the whole time. We examined the bites and found on them the impression of eighteen or twenty teeth, with saliva or spittle all over them in the shape of a mouth, almost all of them very wet, and the spittle [steaming in the cold], as if just spit out of the mouth. I took up some of it on my finger to try the consistency of it, and [another witness] did the same, and we found it clammy like spittle, and it smelt rank.[36]

"Something That Science Cannot Explain"

No source was ever found for the torments suffered by Molly and Dobby, and like many other poltergeist experiences, the troubles ended as mysteriously as they had begun. But in the eighteenth century, few people questioned such events, and poltergeist hauntings were largely considered unpredictable natural occurrences, much the same as hurricanes and earthquakes. It was only in the twentieth century that researchers began to examine the bizarre phenomena with scientific methods. It was also during the last century that people began calling the police when the hauntings started, and in the past 60 years at least 35 police officers from around the world have reported witnessing poltergeist activity. Some have been harmlessly hit by flying objects, and one even pulled his service revolver before realizing that the assault was coming from an invisible force. This leads investigative author Michael Clarkson to write in *Poltergeists*, "[If] we go simply by eyewitness accounts of first-line responders, the officers, even some skeptics may start to suspect there is something paranormal at work here, or at least something that science cannot explain."[37] So while some fill rooms with Tesla coils hoping to re-create ghosts, others continue to view poltergeist events as mysterious forces of nature where half the local graveyard may somehow come alive in order to torment an 11-year-old girl. Whether or not science will ever explain houses haunted by elusive poltergeists remains to be seen.

CHAPTER 4

Hunting the House Haunters

When the comedy movie *Ghostbusters* came out in 1984, it was probably the first time a film was ever made about people who locate ghosts and evict them from haunted houses. But while *Ghostbusters* depicts an exaggerated Hollywood version of apparition stalking, the real job of ghost hunting is much less glamorous. Most who perform the service spend countless hours sitting around in the dark, fighting off sleep, and waiting for spirits to appear. On the odd occasions that ghosts do show up, it is the job of ghost hunters, also called paranormal or psychic investigators, to talk with the phantasms and find out why they are haunting the living. To do so, the investigators use a variety of methods both supernatural and scientific to locate apparitions, follow their activities, and communicate with them.

The actual service performed by ghost hunters can be frustrating or fascinating, depending on the circumstances. Ghosts

generally make contact with the living by shrieking, weeping, wailing, rattling chains, throwing household objects, slamming doors and windows, and emitting disgusting odors. They rarely speak, and if they do, phantoms usually deliver garbled and ambiguous communiqués that only serve to confuse and terrify the living. On occasion, a paranormal investigator may be able to piece together what the apparition is trying to say by studying its life circumstances. For example, a murder victim might want

The blockbuster hit Ghostbusters *made the job of apparition hunting seem dangerous and much more exciting than it actually is.*

to identify her killer, and a person who committed suicide might want to apologize to his mother.

Speaking to a Specter

Those who live in haunted houses are rarely qualified to understand the circumstances surrounding their ghostly manifestation. Frightened residents usually turn to intermediaries, or mediums, to mediate between the living and the dead. Mediums, also called oracles, soothsayers, wizards, witches, shamans, and channelers, act as instruments whereby ghosts can speak to the living. In return, mediums can deliver messages from the physical world to those in the spirit world.

There are three types of mediums. Physical mediums purportedly cause ghosts to materialize or to communicate in the material world. This is often done by inciting the apparition to move objects such as a pencil on paper or a planchette, a heart-shaped piece of wood that either holds a pencil or can be used to spell out messages on an Ouija board.

Another type of medium, called a trance medium, enters a hypnotic, dreamlike state and ostensibly allows a ghost to take over his or her body. In this state, the apparition can write missives by manipulating the medium's hands or speak to observers through the medium's mouth.

The third type of medium, called a mental medium, uses clairvoyance, or "clear seeing," to see ghosts with his or her mind even when the phantoms are not perceived to be physically present. While seeing the ghost in the "mind's eye," mental mediums communicate with the apparitions. Some mediums can do this in a normal, awake mental state, others use crystal balls or some other aid to help them gaze into the otherworld.

Whatever the type of medium, there is no rational explanation for the gift of seeing the supernatural. However, medium Eddie Burks believes that ghosts are attracted to a psychic light or beacon that only channelers emit. Because apparitions are trapped in a particular place, such as a haunted house, they are attracted to this illumination. When they see this psychic light, it acts as a light at the end of a tunnel. The mental beacon draws the ghosts away from where they are ensnared between life and death and allows them to escape their earthly bonds. Burks explains how he knows when his psychic light is active:

> Often a trapped spirit will come to me unbidden; in that case, I sense a change in my mood—I feel uneasy, frustrated or depressed. I know that this feeling does not belong to me because it often happens when I'm feeling quite cheerful. I try to adjust my consciousness to allow [the ghost] to get closer to me; I suppose I bring it into conscious focus. This is not a rational process except that I recognize what is happening mentally. It's more a matter of the heart—I develop an empathy with the spirit. As I focus on it, I begin to find out about the situation; first, I get some idea of whether it's a man or a woman and then I begin to get an understanding of the problem. . . . [It's] as though my intuition—or psychic faculty—reaches out and engages with the entity, but my rational side continues to work so I am able to describe what is happening. It's as though I'm keeping one foot in the real world and one in the psychic world. The

two sides are working together, as the psychic side pulls in information which is filtered through the rational mind.[38]

The Birth of Spiritualism

Mediums like Burks have communicated with ghosts for as long as houses have been haunted. In March 1848, however, the concept of communicating with ghosts became an international fad that put haunted houses—and their ghostly residents—on the front pages of newspapers in the United States and Europe. The craze began innocently in Hydesville, New York, a small town near Rochester, when the Fox family noticed that their house seemed to be haunted. Furniture moved about, and knocking sounds were heard within the walls. One of the young girls who lived in the house, 10-year-old Kate Fox, began communicating with the ghost, asking it to guess the age of her 12-year-old sister, Margaret. The obedient apparition correctly rapped 12 times, and before long the girls developed a code for the phantom to rap out yes or no answers or spell out letters of the alphabet. Their sessions with the resident phantom attracted dozens of neighbors, who watched as the Fox sisters coaxed the entity to reveal that it was the spirit of Charles B. Rosma, a peddler who was murdered in 1843 and was buried in the cellar. Men with shovels were excitedly dispatched to the basement, where a few pieces of bone were exhumed.

A reporter got wind of the story, and after an article appeared in the local paper, it was picked up by the national press. Within weeks, Kate and Margaret Fox were attracting attention from the biggest celebrities of the day, such as circus promoter P.T. Barnum, best-selling author James Fenimore Cooper, and newspaper editor Horace Greeley. Meanwhile, Amy and Isaac Post, two friends of the Fox family from Rochester, started a movement called Spiritualism based on the belief that mediums possessed the ability to communicate with the spirits of the dead. Inspired by the publicity surrounding the Fox sisters, Spiritualism quickly became an international craze. By 1849 countless mediums had gone into business to imitate the Foxes. As the fad spread, just about everyone who believed his or her house might be haunted held a "home circle," or séance, in order to talk to the ghosts.

In a séance, families and friends would gather around a dimly lit table and hold hands. Either a family member or a professional medium would lead a séance, hoping to coax the resident spirits to speak. If members of the home circle were fortunate, an apparition might engage all of their senses. They could feel their séance table tip, smell the perfume of a long-dead woman, hear a loud crash in another room, or see an actual manifestation.

The Phantom Band of the Spirit Room

At the height of the Spiritualism fad, successful mediums attracted hundreds of believers from across the country. This was the case of the Koons family, who lived near present-day Athens, Ohio, in the 1850s in a wilderness that was nearly unreachable except by foot.

Jonathan Koons's haunted house was simply a log cabin built atop Mount Nebo, where he lived with his wife, Abigail, and their nine children. In 1852 Jonathan read a newspaper article about the Fox sisters and began to attend séances in Cleveland, Columbus, and elsewhere. A spirit allegedly told Jonathan that he, his wife, and oldest son, Nahum, had the ability to communicate with

A Code of Ethics
for Ghost Hunters

Ghost hunter Harry Price was well respected for the
ethics he employed while investigating haunted
houses. In *The Most Haunted House in England*, first
published in 1940, Price provides a form for prospec-
tive ghost hunters to sign so that clients can be sure of
their principled intent:

"HAUNTED HOUSE"—DECLARATION FORM

I, the Undersigned, in consideration of having had
my services accepted as an Official Observer, make the
following Declaration. . . .

I will pay my own expenses connected with the investigation.

I am not connected with the Press in any way.

I will not convey to any person the name or location of the alleged Haunted House.

I will not write, nor cause to be written, any account of my visit/s to the Haunted House, and will not lecture on my experiences there.

I will not photograph or sketch any part of the Haunted House or grounds without written permission. . . .

I will not use the Telephone installed in the House except for the purpose of reporting phenomena to the person or persons whose names have been given me, or for requesting assistance from those persons.

I will lock all doors and fasten all windows on my leaving the House, and will deposit key/s to person as directed.

Harry Price, *The Most Haunted House in England.* London: Longmans, Green, 1990, p. 193.

the dead. Upon returning home, Jonathan held several séances in his cabin, and a resident ghost told him to build a "Spirit Room" next to his cabin. The ghost must have been quite a builder because it specified the exact size, 12 by 14 feet (3.6 by 4.2m), told the Koons the location of the three windows, and also instructed the family on how to furnish the room with benches to hold 20 visitors. The spirit also requested that the room be stocked with musical instruments, including drums, fiddles, a guitar, an accordion, a trumpet, a tin horn, a triangle, a tambourine, and a bell. In addition, bells were to be suspended from the ceiling along with sculptures of doves cut from copper sheeting.

After investing considerable time and money in the Spirit Room, Jonathan, Abigail, and Nahum began giving séances in the dark cabin. During these meetings, spirits would purportedly appear and give long talks meant to enlighten observers about the world of the haunted. The apparitions followed their lectures with concerts. Jonathan, channeling a ghost called John King, led the orchestra on the fiddle while other instruments were played by invisible hands. The phantom band played songs that were unfamiliar to observers but were said to be melodic. Sometimes unseen voices sang, but the words were not in English.

Reports of the time say that the ghost music could be heard up to 1 mile (1.6km) away, and the Spirit Room actually shook from the ear-splitting volume of the songs. The banging of the bass drum alone was compared to the sound of a cannon. Witnesses also claim that as the songs gained in intensity, the instruments lifted into the air and circled the room. Astounded visitors looked on as trumpets, drums, and triangles emitted songs while flying by their faces, sometimes striking them or landing in their laps. Then, as suddenly as it began, the phantom concert would draw to a close. In the grand finale to each séance, armless hands appeared in the air and furiously began writing messages on pieces of paper at amazing speeds.

It did not take long for news of the ghost band to attract widespread interest. On any given night up to 50 people could be found in the Spirit Room gladly offering donations to hear the ghostly speeches and songs. As the attention increased, so too did the claims of John King, who said he commanded 165 spirits who were inhabiting the house.

The Koons family operated the Spirit Room for several years; during that time, dozens of professional skeptics, reporters, religious authorities, and politicians vouched to the authenticity of the ghostly band and writing events. In 1858, however, Jonathan Koons announced that John King had left the building and his tin horn would play no more.

Professionalizing the Ghost Trade

The Koons family was often accused of perpetuating a hoax on gullible believers, but they did not charge for their séances and never got rich from the donations. Other mediums, however, did charge for their services, and they were most often hired by grieving families who wished to communicate with the ghosts of their dead relatives. By the end of the nineteenth century nearly every town had several professional channelers who might use sleight of hand, carnival tricks, theatrical lighting, and costumed assistants to create the illusion of a haunting.

In 1882 a group of serious parapsychologists in England founded the Society for Psychical Research (SPR) in order to separate legitimate ghost-hunting activities from the fraudulent activities of many mediums. The SPR included some of London's most elite

citizens, including author Lewis Carroll, poet Lord Tennyson, and prime minister William Gladstone. The goal of the organization was to professionalize ghost hunting by providing scientific guidelines for locating, communicating with, and exorcizing apparitions. The SPR's official guidelines categorized ghostly manifestations such as noises, odors, physical contact, movement of an object, and appearances. Investigators were told to be skeptical, keep an open mind, and check every possible source for the haunting. Sites were to be investigated during different weather conditions, during the day, and at night.

Members of the SPR developed ghost-locating techniques that are still in use. For example, to ascertain if an apparition was walking about a haunted house, SPR members sprinkled flour on the floor to detect phantom footprints. In order to determine if an apparition was moving furniture or other objects with an unseen hand, investigators recommended using chalk to draw rings around furniture legs and objects on tables.

Tools and Methods for Hunting Ghosts

The techniques developed by the SPR were crucial to those hunting phantoms in haunted houses for nearly 50 years. In the late 1920s, however, British investigator Harry Price moved ghost hunting into a new era by employing tools such as highly accurate thermometers to detect slight temperature variations caused by ghosts entering or leaving a room. And when investigating a haunted house, Price packed recently invented remote-controlled cameras for indoor and outdoor ghost photography. Most importantly, Price published a pamphlet called *The Blue Book: Instructions for Observers,* which was a compilation of the knowledge he had gathered investigating dozens of haunted houses.

The Blue Book offers a list of tools ghost hunters should pack, the types of phenomena to watch for, and methods for dealing with curious onlookers and the press. In the tool section, Price recommends each investigator bring a "notebook, pencils, good watch with second hand, candle and matches, electric torch [flashlight], brandy flask, sandwiches, etc. If he possess a camera, this can be used. Rubber or felt-soled shoes should be worn."[39]

In *The Blue Book*, Price explains how to scientifically investigate a haunted house. First, all doors and windows should be locked, nailed shut, or sealed with tape to prevent tampering by the living. The house should be patrolled throughout the hunt, and each room, along with the grounds, should be visited hourly. When the ghost hunter is outdoors, he or she should observe windows from the exterior of the building in order to spot ghosts lurking about the rooms. Price recommends occasionally extinguishing all lights and waiting in total stillness in the dark for ghosts to appear. Ghost hunters should also leave time to fill out detailed hourly reports in order to "make the fullest notes of the slightest unusual sound or occurrence."[40]

After discussing various ghost-hunting methods, Price goes on to describe typical spectral phenomena an investigator might encounter. At a time when many old mansions had bells in the ceiling attached to long ropes that could be pulled to summon a butler, ghosts were apparently fond of ringing these bells to attract attention. The movement of objects is another phantasm phenomenon, and Price has seen everything from matchboxes to furniture flying through the air in haunted houses. In such cases, Price advises investigators to draw up a rough floor plan of the room and record the direction of movement. If the object is seen, the speed, trajectory, and force of movement should be noted. Other phenomena include mysterious lights, temperature changes, raps or knocks, and objects appearing and disappearing. If any of the above events are observed, Price tells investigators to make sure they are not "due to normal causes, such as rats, small boys, the villagers, the wind, wood shrinking, the [wood-boring] beetle, farm animals nosing the doors . . . [or] birds in the chimney-stack."[41]

On rare occasions, ghost hunters will actually encounter their quarry in visible form. In such cases, Price recommends responding scientifically rather than emotionally. Psychic investigators should note all ghostly movements, whether the apparition is solid or transparent, the duration of the appearance, and the color, form, size, and type of clothing. Ghost hunters may try to take a picture of the phantasm but not speak until spoken to. If the ghost is in a talkative mood, Price writes:

> *[Do] not approach*, but ascertain name, age, sex, origin, cause of visit, if in trouble, and possible alleviation. Inquire if it is a spirit. Ask figure to return, suggesting exact time and place. Do not move until the figure disappears. Note exact method of vanishing. If through an open door, quietly follow. If through solid object (such as wall) ascertain if still visible on other side. Make the very fullest notes of the incident.[42]

The Borley Rectory

Price developed his ghost hunting techniques during the course of a long, eventful career investigating haunted houses, beginning in 1920 when he joined the SPR. These methods proved particularly useful to Price during his ongoing investigation of the Borley Rectory, recognized as the most haunted house in England, and possibly the world.

The Borley Rectory was a sprawling Victorian building located near the small town of Borley in rural Essex. It was close to the twelfth-century Borley Church and was built on a site where at least two other buildings, including a fourteenth-century monastery, once stood. Although Price began his investigation of the rectory in 1929, the Borley Rectory had a reputation for being haunted since it was first constructed in 1863.

A rectory is a house in which a parish priest or rector lives, often with his family, but the Borley Rectory was said to house otherworldly guests as well. Local legend has it that the grounds were haunted by a beautiful young nun who had a love affair with a monk in the 1500s. When the couple tried to elope in a black coach on a full-moon night, they were chased by unidentified forces, captured, and returned to the church. The monk was hanged, and the nun was entombed alive within the walls of the monastery. Another variant of the story has the monk strangling his lover after a quarrel.

Although the veracity of the story has been called into question by historians, according to Price, there is little doubt that the nun's ghost has been haunting the rectory for many years:

> The nun has been seen many times by many people, and the evidence is incontrovertible. She has been seen walking, standing under a tree, gliding along the [path called the] Nun's Walk, and leaning over a gate. She has been seen as a typical Sister of Mercy, a somber figure, a shadow, and as

a substantial young woman attired in typical nun's clothing. She has been seen by individuals singly, by two persons together, and once by four persons simultaneously . . . proving that the figure was objective. She has been seen to vanish spontaneously. . . . She has been seen in daylight, by moonlight, and at dawn—four times by one man, on different occasions.[43]

A Yearlong Hunt for Spirits

Price first investigated the Borley Rectory in June 1929, after he was notified by a reporter of the bizarre events taking place there. In addition to the nun sightings, the home's occupants, the Reverend G.E. Smith and his wife, reported hearing odd noises such as footsteps dragging across the floor and a woman's voice shrieking. Smith also reported seeing strange lights in the windows from outdoors along with a headless coachman driving a phantom coach. The ghostly events were seemingly harmless, but the Smiths moved out as Price was beginning his investigation. When the new residents, the Reverend Lionel Foyster and his wife, Marianne, moved in, in 1930, the ghostly activities increased dramatically. On some nights, while the couple cringed under the bed sheets, windows shattered, furniture was loudly dragged from room to room, and piercing knocks echoed through the house. The apparition seemed to take particular delight in tormenting Marianne, who was pulled from her bed, slapped by phantom hands, and was forced to dodge heavy objects that were thrown at her day and night. Then written messages from an unknown source began to appear on the walls, pleading for her help and instructing Marianne to light candles for prayers.

Before it was demolished in 1944, the Borley Rectory was recognized as the most haunted house in England, and possibly the world. It had a reputation for being haunted since it was first constructed in 1863.

After several months of such events, the Foysters left the Borley Rectory and the building sat abandoned for several years. Price, who had never seen written messages purported to be from apparitions, finally rented the rectory in 1937 and began a yearlong, round-the-clock investigation. During the course of the year he was visited by several scholars from the SPR, a military officer, a doctor's assistant, and a journalist from the British Broadcasting Corporation. Every one of these observers verified that hundreds of ghostly events were occurring within the rectory.

The most common incidents involved furniture, decorations, and knickknacks being moved either a few inches or a few feet. Sometimes this happened while an observer was in the room but was not looking. Investigators also reported a nearly constant barrage of odd noises, including clicks, thumps, taps, footsteps, and crashes that sounded like dishes falling in the kitchen. Puddles of brown water and gluelike substances appeared and disappeared suddenly, and foul odors similar to a backed up toilet sickened several ghost hunters.

A Murdered Nun in the Ruins

Although Price and his observers thoroughly recorded the activities in their notebooks, they were unable to communicate with the spirits that apparently haunted the rectory. Frustrated by the lack of contact, Price decided to return to ghost hunting basics and hold a séance using a planchette to spell out the details of the haunting. With eight hands lightly touching the planchette, a spirit named Marie Lairre visited the séance participants and spelled out the story of her death in the seventeenth century.

Lairre said that she was a French nun who left her convent to marry Henry Waldegrave, a member of a wealthy family whose manor home once stood on the site of the rectory. The short, unhappy marriage came to an abrupt halt when Waldegrave strangled Lairre and buried her remains in the cellar. Lairre told the assembled ghost hunters that she continued to haunt the rectory because she wanted her bones to be exhumed and moved to a cemetery, buried with a requiem mass conducted by a Catholic priest. Price concluded that Lairre was trying to communicate her wishes to Marianne Foyster in the messages that the apparition had written about a mass and prayers. He concluded that the nun would haunt the rectory forever unless her request was fulfilled.

Price searched the rectory basement for bones, but none were recovered. Hoping to find an answer to this mystery, the ghost hunter held another séance with the planchette five months later, in March 1938. This time a phantasm that called himself Sunex Amures appeared. In clipped language, he told the assembled observers, "Mean to burn the rectory to-night at 9 o'clock end of the haunting go to the rectory and you will be able to . . . find bone of murdered [nun] under the ruins . . . you will have proof of haunting of the rectory at Borley . . . [which] tells the story of murder which happened there."[44]

The rectory did not burn that night, nor did Price find any bones. But exactly 11 months later, after a new tenant, Captain W.H. Gregson moved in, the Borley Rectory burned to the ground. In the following months, World War II broke out, and Price did not return to the rectory to search for Lairre's skeletal remains until 1943. He found several fragile human bones under the brick floor in the cellar, gave them a proper burial, and no further hauntings were reported at the ruins of the rectory, which was finally demolished by townspeople in 1944.

Since that time, Price's 2 books about the haunting, *The Most Haunted House in England* and *The End of Borley Rectory* (1946), have acted as guides for psychic researchers throughout

Written messages from an unknown source began to appear on the walls of the Borley Rectory, pleading for help and instructing the residents to light candles for prayers.

Marianne
light mass
prayers

Marann
Please hel
get

Marianne

I CANNOT UNDERSTAND
TELL ME MORE

Marianne.

I STILL. CANNOT UNDERSTAND
PLEASE. TELL ME MORE.

the world. Today there are thousands of ghost hunters across the globe. They even have their own professional organization, the International Ghost Hunters Society, which claims 14,000 members in 87 countries. In the twenty-first century digital recorders, computers, high-tech thermometers, and sensitive electronic instruments such as EMF meters and radio frequency counters have replaced chalk and box cameras. But the hauntings persist as spirits from the past continue to make house calls and defy attempts to document, or even explain, their presence.

NOTES

Introduction: Home Not Alone

1. Sir Edward Bulwer-Lytton, *The Haunted and the Haunters*, Bartleby Books, 2005. www.bartleby.com.

2. St. John D. Seymour and Harry L. Neligan, *True Irish Ghost Stories*. New York: Barnes & Noble, 2003, p. 1.

Chapter 1: Who Haunts Houses?

3. Prince Michael of Greece, *Living with Ghosts*. New York: W.W. Norton, 1996, p. 13.

4. Marc Alexander, *Phantom Britain*. London: Frederick Muller, 1975, p. 14.

5. Quoted in James Houran and Rense Lange, eds., *Hauntings and Poltergeists*. Jefferson, NC: McFarland, 2001, pp. 41–42.

6. Quoted in Alexander, *Phantom Britain*, p. 18.

7. Quoted in Alexander, *Phantom Britain*, p. 18.

8. Quoted in Alexander, *Phantom Britain*, p. 18.

9. Hans Holzer, *Ghosts: True Encounters with the World Beyond*. New York: Black Dog & Leventhal, 1997, p. 667.

10. Holzer, *Ghosts*, p. 667.

11. Holzer, *Ghosts*, p. 669.

12. Quoted in Houran and Lange, *Hauntings and Poltergeists*, p. 125.

13. Quoted in Steve Cox, "Plato on Demons," Ibiblio, March 24, 1998. www.ibiblio.org.

14. SilverRain Queen, "Characteristics of a Demon Haunting: Is There a Demon in Your House?" Unexplained-Mysteries, November 4, 2006. www.unexplained-mysteries. com.

15. Queen, "Characteristics of a Demon Haunting."

Chapter 2: Real Haunted Houses

16. Holzer, *Ghosts*, p. 234.

17. Pliny the Younger, "Letters," Bartleby Books, 2007. www. bartleby. com.

18. Pliny the Younger, "Letters."

19. Quoted in Alexander, *Phantom Britain*, p. 39.

20. Edgar Allan Poe, "The Premature Burial," Read Easily, 2007. www.readeasily.com.

21. Quoted in Arthur Myers, *The Ghostly Register*. New York: Dorset, 1986, p. 158.

22. Quoted in Myers, *The Ghostly Register*, p. 160.

Chapter 3: Nasty, Noisy, Horrific Hauntings

23. Joseph Braddock, *Haunted Houses of Great Britain*. New York: Dorset, 1991, p. 87.

24. Quoted in Braddock, *Haunted Houses of Great Britain*, p. 82.

25. Quoted in Holzer, *Ghosts*, p. 672.

26. Quoted in Holzer, *Ghosts*, p. 674.

27. Quoted in Holzer, *Ghosts*, p. 675.

28. Quoted in Holzer, *Ghosts*, p. 675.

29. Quoted in Holzer, *Ghosts*, p. 688.

30. Holzer, *Ghosts*, p. 689.

31. Quoted in Michael Clarkson, *Poltergeists*. Buffalo, NY: Firefly, 2005, p. 23.

32. Colin Wilson, *Poltergeist: A Study in Destructive Haunting*. St. Paul, MN: Llewellyn, 1993, pp. 256–57.

33. Quoted in Guy Playfair, *This House Is Haunted*. New York: Stein and Day, 1980, pp. 142–43.

34. Quoted in Wilson, *Poltergeist*, p. 264.

35. Quoted in Herbert Thurston, *Ghosts and Poltergeists*. Chicago: H. Regnery, 1954, p. 38.

36. Quoted in D. Scott Rogo, *The Poltergeist Experience: Investigations into Ghostly Phenomena*. New York: Penguin, 1979, p. 183.

37. Clarkson, *Poltergeists*, p. 10.

Chapter 4: Hunting the House Haunters

38. Eddie Burks and Gillian Cribb, *Ghosthunter*. London: Headline, 1995, pp. 23–24.

39. Harry Price, *The Most Haunted House in England*. London: Longmans, Green, 1990, p. 194.

40. Price, *The Most Haunted House in England*, p. 194.

41. Price, *The Most Haunted House in England*, p. 197.

42. Price, *The Most Haunted House in England*, p. 196.

43. Price, *The Most Haunted House in England*, p. 32.

44. Quoted in Price, *The Most Haunted House in England*, p. 164.

For Further Research

Books

Michael Clarkson, *Poltergeists: Examining Mysteries of the Paranormal*. Buffalo, NY: Firefly, 2006. A study of numerous hauntings, including an 11-year-old boy inhabited by a poltergeist and a 14-year-old girl whose haunted house causes her to make objects float and crash to the ground.

Denice Jones, *The Other Side: The True Story of the Boy Who Sees Ghosts*. Far Hills, NJ: New Horizon, 2000. Written by his mother, this story tells the story of 10-year-old Michael who lived in a haunted house where he witnessed many diabolical events that plagued both him and his relatives.

Prince Michael of Greece, *Living with Ghosts*. New York: W.W. Norton, 1996. Eleven tales of the rich and haunted, written by the grandson of King George I of Greece about his visits to ghost-infested castles, chateaus, and palaces.

Terry O'Neill, ed., *Haunted Houses*. San Diego: Greenhaven, 2004. An examination of haunted houses, with chapters by believers, investigators, scientists, and skeptics discussing paranormal events and ghostly manifestations.

David West, *Ghosts and Poltergeists: Stories of the Supernatural*. New York: Rosen, 2006. This work includes chapters about the world of ghosts, the Macomb poltergeist, the Amityville Horror, and other phantasmic haunts.

Anne Wilder, *House of Spirits and Whispers: The True Story of a Haunted House*. St. Paul, MN: Llewellyn, 2005. A gripping tale about living in a 100-year-old house where disembodied voices, pounding walls, glowing lights, and visiting ghosts terrified the author and her family.

Web Sites

Harry Price: Ghost-Hunter, Psychical Researcher, and Author (http://harryprice.co.uk). The official Web site of the world's most famous ghost hunter, with links to photographs, books by and about Price, and famous cases, including the Borley Rectory.

The Haunters and the Haunted (www.bartleby.com/166). This site, hosted by Bartleby Books, offers 57 classic stories of ghosts and hauntings from literary works, local records, folklore, and myth.

Real Haunted Houses (www.realhaunts.com). An extensive resource of haunted houses, spooky stories, ghostly tales, and other paranormal events.

The Shadowlands Haunted Places Index (http://theshadowlands.net/places). An index of haunted places in nearly every state in the United States along with an extensive country-by-country list of haunted houses, schools, churches, roads, and other sites throughout the world.

Zerotime Paranormal Publishing (www.zerotime.com/ghosts). This Web site provides information about ghosts, ghost hunters, myths and legends, poltergeist activity, and even voice recordings of alleged phantoms.

INDEX

A

Adams, Abigail, 47
Adams, John, 47
agents, 50–51
Alexander, Marc, 14
animals
    behavior toward ghosts, 20, 26
    as ghosts, 48, 64
Athenodorus, 30
Athens, Greece, 29–31
Australia, 8

B

Baltimore, MD, 44–45
Barnum, P.T., 72
Beaird family haunting
    behavior of Johnnie, 51
    bug raids, 51–52, 54–56
    explanation, 59–60
    fires, 53
    furniture moved, 57–58
    notes found, 55, 56–57
    voices, 53–54
Bierce, Ambrose, 24–25
Blue Book: Instructions for Observers (Price), 78–80
Blunded, Edward, 18
Boleyn, Anne, 37
Borley Rectory, Great Britain, 81–85
Braddock, Joseph, 49–50
bug raids, 51–52, 54–56, 61
Bulwer-Lytton, Sir Edward, 7
burials
    in ancient Greece, 30–31
    Dickie, 31, 34–35
    Lairre, 84–85
Burks, Eddie, 71–72

C

Cage, Nicholas, 43
California, 32–33
Carroll, Lewis, 78
cat hauntings, 48
channelers
    Janet Harper, 64–65
    Jonathan Koons, 76
    mediums as, 70
    psychic light emitted by, 71–72
Charles I (king of England), 39
Christopher (prince of Greece), 12
clairvoyance, 70
Clarkson, Michael, 58–59, 67
clothing, 24–25
communication
    rules for ghost hunters, 80
    through mediums, 70
    verbal, 69
    written messages, 55, 56–57, 77, 82
Cooper, James Fenimore, 72

D

deaths
    caused by ghosts, 17, 18
    hauntings resulting from, 28, 41
demons
    ancient, 22
    behavior, 22–23
    exorcism to remove, 22, 23
    hauntings, 24–27
    in Windsor Castle, 39
Derbyshire, Great Britain, 31, 34–35
Devil's Dictionary (Bierce), 24–25
Dickie (spirit), 31, 34–35
Dickson, Ned, 34
dogs
    behavior toward ghosts, 20, 26
    as ghosts, 64
Dupre (ghost), 16–18
Durbin, Henry, 65, 66

E

echo effect, 14
electrical emanations, 14
electricity, 60–61
Elizabeth I (queen of England), 39
End of Borley Rectory, The (Price), 85, 87
Enfield, Great Britain, 63–65
Estes family, 20
Evans, Hillary, 15–16
evil houses, 16–18
exorcism
    of demons, 22, 23
    in New Guinea, 8
    in Pennsylvania, 27
    in Siberia, 8
explanations
    electrical emanations, 14

About the Author

Stuart A. Kallen is a prolific author who has written more than 200 nonfiction books for children and young adults over the past 20 years. His books have covered countless aspects of human history, culture, and science, from the building of the pyramids to the music of the twenty-first century. Some of his recent titles include *History of World Music*, *Romantic Art*, and *Women of the Civil Rights Movement*. Kallen is also an accomplished singer-songwriter and guitarist in San Diego, California.